To: _____

From: _____

Mom

Published by Sellers Publishing, Inc.
Copyright © 2010 Sellers Publishing, Inc.
Photography © 2010 Kendra Dew
All rights reserved.

Edited by Robin Haywood

161 John Roberts Road, South Portland, Maine 04106
For ordering information:
(800) 625-3386 Toll free
(207) 772-6814 Fax
Visit our Web site: www.sellerspublishing.com
E-mail: rsp@rsvp.com

ISBN: 13: 978-1-4162-0567-8

10 9 8 7 6 5 4 3 2 1

Printed and bound in China.

Mom

WHAT WOULD I DO WITHOUT SOMEONE LIKE YOU?

PHOTOGRAPHY BY KENDRA DEW

SELLERS
PUBLISHING

Mom, remember when you taught me to laugh?

to love?

*to appreciate life's
simple pleasures?*

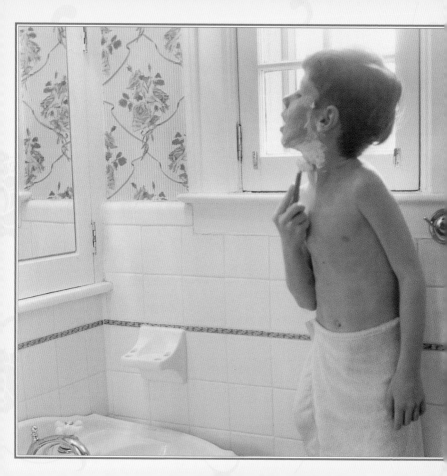

A day doesn't go by when
I don't say or do something
you taught me.

From you, I learned the world is full of magic,

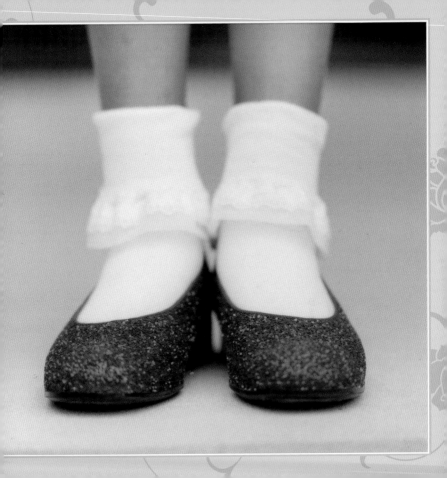

and delight,

and wonder — if I just know where to look.

You taught me to be brave,

and strong,

and fearless.

You encouraged me to follow my dreams and listen to my heart.

From you, I learned there's nothing I can't be,

even if it's a fairy princess.

I learned about love,

and sharing,

and happiness.

You taught me the value of friendship

and how to express myself!

You've always been there to listen.

You showed me the importance of making my own way in the world.

*You never gave
up on me,
Mom.*

You were always there with a kind word and a hug, just when I needed it the most.

*I have always felt
loved and protected.*

My future is bright,
and I owe it to you.

You teach by example and nurture with love,

*and what you've taught me
about life, I will pass on
to my children.*

Mom, thank you for being there and for believing in me.

You're the original superhero!

Without you there
would be no me.

I am who I am because of you.